AIR TO AIR

BY JOHN M. DIBBS

Cover: USAF F-22 Raptor of the 302nd FS from Elmendorf AFB over an Alaskan Glacier.

This page: Air Superiority. It's not just a phrase, it's a state of mind. An Eagle of the 199th FS HI ANG unleashes magnesium flares off Hawaii.

For my family — My late Dad, John Snr, whose memory and values still inspire me, my loving Mum and my sister Claire.

Special thanks and gratitude to the owners, pilots, engineers, office managers and staff who made these flights possible. Pam Dibbs, whose amazing organisational skills have made the 1,000 sorties happen.

Also I would like to thank the following for their support: The great warbird collections and the people behind them — The Fighter Collection, The Old Flying Machine Company, The Aircraft Restoration Co, Frasca Air Museum, Flying Heritage Collection — Dennis Neville, who was my first ever shoot subject, Allan Burney, who gave me valuable critique of that first shoot and has been following up with more since (joke), Nicky Hall at Check Six, Lynne Isted at Virgin Atlantic, Andy Patsalides, Kurt Peterson, Adrian Hunt, Mike Gurley at Canon, Jim, Bob and Scott Donovan at Kenmore Camera, Adina Preston at TPPC, Tim Ellison, Norman Lees, 'Punch' Churchill, 'Cricket' Renner, 'Nubes' Neubauer, and all those who have served and those serving.

Keep dreaming, it's all possible…

All colour photography: © 2015 John M. Dibbs

Concept and design: © 2015 John M. Dibbs and Adina Preston

Layout and pre-production: John M. Dibbs and Adina Preston

Production: The Plane Picture Company and Narcosis Media

www.planepicture.com | www.facebook.com/theplanepicture

KEY PUBLISHING

Publisher and Managing Director Adrian Cox. **Executive Chairman** Richard Cox.
Commercial Director Ann Saundry. **Editor** Allan Burney.

Distribution (UK) Seymour Distribution Ltd, 2 Poultry Avenue, London +44 (0)20 7429 4000

Printing Precision Colour Printing Ltd, Halesfield 1, Telford, Shropshire, TF7 4QQ

All rights reserved. The entire content of 'Air-to-Air' is © Key Publishing 2015. Reproduction in whole or in part and in any form whatsoever is strictly prohibited without the prior permission of the Publisher. We are unable to guarantee the bona fides of any of our advertisers. Readers are strongly recommended to take their own precautions before parting with any information or item of value, including, but not limited to, money, manuscripts, photographs or personal information in response to any advertisements within this publication.

Published by Key Publishing Ltd, PO Box 100, Stamford, Lincs PE19 1XQ.

Tel: +44 (0) 1780 755131. Fax: +44 (0) 1780 757261.

Website: www.keypublishing.com

ISBN (UK): 9781910415375

CONTENTS

INTRODUCTION 6

ACES & LEGENDS 8

ADRENALINE JUNKIES 42

INTO THE BLUE 50

WIND IN THE WIRES 66

GODS OF THUNDER 74

"There's a Spitfire hanging off our wing tip, its propeller practically chewing off the end of my lens. The roar of the mighty Merlin is resonating through my gut like a power drill and the slipstream from the open door is beating up what's left of me. I wait patiently for the stars to align. Sunlight begins to dance off the virtuous form of the Spitfire and without warning the ground plummets away in a vertigo-inducing display of beauty to reveal a backdrop of crisp white cliffs set against an azure blue sea. Click. Mission accomplished. The shot is in the can. I remember to start breathing again..."

'If it lifts off the rail, push this button'. So said Wilbur Wright to John Thomas Daniels Jr, a life guard working on a blustery day at Kill Devil Hill, Kittyhawk, North Carolina on 17 December 1903. We know the 'it' (the 'Wright Flyer'), did lift off the rail because John Thomas Daniels Jr did push the button and that released the shutter on a tripod-mounted camera, thereby capturing the moment mankind achieved the millennia-old dream of powered flight for the first time ever. Thus, in one fell swoop aviation and aviation photography were borne… and to my mind, that very first image is still one of the most powerful ever taken. The intensity of the moment is palpable thanks to Wilbur's body language as he watches Orville actually take to the skies, the weak winter shadow cast upon the windy North Carolina sands proved that man had left the surface of the planet under power, the front elevators at full deflection show the machine's struggle to attain the previously impossible.

This has become my mantra in my work, i.e. to capture the moment in the best, most honest and dramatic way I know. Much like John T Daniels Jr, who was handed the shutter release, I too have been fortunate in being in the right time and place to discover a passion that has driven me for 25 years. I have also had the good fortune of knowing and learning from some legends of the aviation and photography business upon the way.

Growing up I was inspired by the beautiful imagery of Charles Brown, but I was also fortunate to have met and worked with one of the true greats of aviation photography Arthur Gibson. Arthur, whose highly-original work is sadly overlooked these days, changed my life completely by offering to take me on an air-to-air sortie. It was to be an inauspicious start as I didn't even see the other aircraft due to my head being buried in a bag! But Arthur continued to encourage me and instilled a desire to beat whatever obstacles lay in my way. He passed away several years back, but his spirit is packed in my camera bag every time I go flying. Another photo-great who proved to be a trusted and great friend was George Hall. Known mainly for his 'Top Gun' work, he too was a pioneer. Sadly George has gone now, taken way too early, but there isn't a time when I am aloft in an Eagle when I don't think of him. George was the humble Jedi master, looking after a whole generation of photographers. The final piece in my inspiration puzzle is Katsuhiko Tokunaga. The Japanese magician raised the game, creating images of immense drama and dynamism. He is another true gentleman of the profession.

◀ The Wright Flyer, 17 December 1903

INTRODUCTION

But air-to-air photography is far more than just about the man behind the lens, it is all about teamwork. The photographer and his camera only get aloft if you have a camera-ship pilot and an aircraft to shoot! As far as teamwork goes this is a pretty high stakes game and so knowing the players is vital. Trust is the key word in formation flying. The formating pilot needs to trust the lead, the lead ship crew, including me, needs to trust the pilot flying feet off our wing, and they both need to trust that I won't do anything to compromise the flying. As such, I have been fortunate to work with some incredibly talented people.

For the past few years I have flown almost exclusively with Tim Ellison as my camera-ship pilot. Tim is an amazing person on many levels. His visual-spatial skills are immense, honed as a Harrier pilot in the RAF, and his airmanship second to none. The other inspiring thing about working with Tim is that he was injured in a flying accident when his Harrier's engine failed him at a crucial point. He has been in a wheelchair since and after many years of rehabilitation he got back flying using levers instead of pedals. I think the bond between Tim and I is that we both find a rare freedom in the skies. We share a mental datalink airborne, so if you look through this volume and a photo stirs something in you, then thank Tim as much as me.

Then there are the pilots on the wing. I am extremely lucky to have worked with some of the World's top pilots. Stephen and Nick Grey are amazing either air-to-air or if you are watching from the ground. Mark and Ray Hanna were both greats of the display circuit, as was Hoof Proudfoot and Norman Lees. John Romain is not only a great engineer, but a pilot of outstanding experience and a great camera-ship pilot too. Steve Hinton is, well Steve Hinton. One of the best and nicest blokes to work with. That's just warbirds. In the fast jet World I have met some great pilots who put their bodies and futures on the line in the name of their country. 'Punch' Churchill has been a real source of inspiration, 'Cricket' Renner another top bloke. With over 1,000 sorties under my belt, I cannot mention everyone, but to all I am eternally grateful.

However, there is one final person to whom I own an enormous debt… my father. It was his drive and passion that set in motion my interest in photography and aviation and for that I am ever grateful. This publication is dedicated to his memory and my family.

Fly High!

Dibbsy

What kit do I take into the skies?

I have always used Canon gear. The EOS system is tough, durable and reliable. If these little boxes of tricks go wrong, then the whole effort is rendered pointless, so I need to trust my kit. I currently use Canon EOS 1Dx and Canon EOS 5D Mark III. My aerial Canon lenses are the 24-70 f2.8L and 70-200 f2.8L II.

ACES & LEGENDS

AIRCRAFT FROM THE GREATEST GENERATION

If ever the soul were to be stirred by the art of shaped and formed metal, then there can be no finer contenders than the aircraft from the Second World War period. Stephen Grey of 'The Fighter Collection' once referred to them as the last of the gladiatorial steeds. He was right.

Previous Page

Full on with the Flying Bulls F4U-4 Corsair. Face-to-face with the bent-wing bird, Eric Goujon, a former Mirage 2000 pilot, shows us why we should keep warbirds in the skies.

◀

Hangar 11 Heaven! This image represents the very essence of what I endeavour to capture. Peter Teichman, the main man behind the North Weald-based Hangar 11, has a penchant for authenticity, you can see it and sense it around his aircraft. He wanted a photograph of all four of his immaculate warbirds in formation. As you can imagine, it wasn't a cheap exercise so the pressure was on! Tim Ellison flew the camera-ship smooth as smooth could be, like pushing a cat on ice-skates. Any bump from the leader is magnified four times by the end of the line of aircraft, which would have ruined the perfect shot that Peter wanted. It's not easy calculating all that 'up and down, back and forth' to look just right. The four pilots, Pete in the P-40, Maurice Hammond in the P-51, Stu Goldspink in the Hurri-bomber and Steve Jones in the Spitfire Mk XI did an epic job.

Peter Teichman tickling our tail feathers with his prop. Rock solid.

◀

'Glacier Girl'. The P-38 looks like something from the future even now. Backlit the essence of its genius is evident. Legendary designer Clarence 'Kelly' Johnson thought outside the box that's for sure. Steve Hinton comes in for a closer look at the camera over Middlesboro Kentucky, original home of the 'Glacier Girl'.

▶

'Twin-tailed devil' was the Luftwaffe's nickname for the P-38. Here we chase the Flying Bulls' example above the clouds. Gleaming in the afternoon sun the machine shows its unique planform.

◀

Gripping Griffon. Some pilot and aircraft combinations are unbeatable. Phill O'Dell, Rolls-Royce's Chief Pilot, unhindered by the lack of cockpit struts on the pressurized Spitfire Mk XIX's cockpit, as well as a lifetime of experience, has an instinct for getting the shot in the can. As you might imagine, Rolls' mighty Griffon engine output is pulsating and can be felt through your chest even in the camera-ship!

▲ Painted in the colours of P/O Billy Fiske, No 601 Squadron RAF, Biggin Hill Heritage Hangar's Hurricane Mk I is a poignant reminder of the sacrifice of those gone before. Billy Fiske was 'the first American to die so that England might live', as quoted on a memorial in St Paul's Cathedral to him, lost from injuries sustained in the Battle of Britain. UF-K is bathed in glorious light over the Thames Estuary, with Richard Grace at the controls.

ACES & LEGENDS | 15

◀

Eight Merlins in perfect harmony. The summer of 2014 was the time of the Lancaster Pair. The duo was a huge success and crowds all over the UK got to see the Battle of Britain Memorial Flight Lancaster fly with the Canadian Warplane Heritage example at shows across the country. Formating alongside these two awesome machines was one of those 'pinch yourself' moments. 'Awesome' is an over used word, but it was the only way to describe it. Ironically, seeing two Lancasters only made one wonder what six hundred might have looked like.

▶

There are few finer exponents of the art of display or formation flying than Stephen Grey. His passion for World War 2 aviation is unparalleled. I was lucky enough to have one of my first ever air-to-air shoots with Stephen and we have flown together many times since. He is a great collector of art and his appreciation of aesthetics shows in his display flying. Now despite this appreciation of 'artistry', he does like to keep shoots 'efficient'; I even have a photo of him pointing at his watch in the cockpit! Here is Stephen in Spitfire Mk IX ML417. Now is that the Merlin growling or Stephen?

▲

The Shuttleworth Collection Sea Hurricane Mk I. Despite being a 'Sea Hurri', this image always makes me feel like it is the view that so many of 'The Few' would have had of their leader desperately climbing to make height during the Battle of Britain.

◄

A Perfect Pair. John Romain and Lee Proudfoot have flown together from their earliest days, so how fitting that they should be seen here flying the earliest Spitfires airworthy. This shoot was taken on a very tight deadline and the pressure was on. It was only while looking at the images later that I realised quite what had taken place. A lifetime's ambition, that's all!

◀

A Japanese Zero caught against a waning sun. How poignant can that be? This image was one of the first of the digital era when I realised that photography had entered a new dimension. Steve Barber is the very highly skilled pilot behind the stick. He flies many of the amazing types operated by the SoCal CAF Wing, which is well worth a pit stop if you are travelling up the Pacific Coast Highway near Camarillo.

▶

Sir Tim Wallis championed the warbird movement in New Zealand, deep in Lord of the Rings country long before Orcs and Hobbits lived there. Here he is in 1994 flying his Spitfire Mk XVI around Mount Aspiring in the Southern Alps. As we crested a ridge, I remarked to my pilot, 'now I know where the angels live'. He in a typical Kiwi retort said: 'Yes its very pretty, but if the engine stops now, put your head between your legs and kiss your arse goodbye as there's no out from here.'

◀

The business end of a 'Butcher Bird'. Steve Hinton in Flying Heritage Collection's genuine FW190. I originally saw this aircraft in the UK immediately post recovery from Russia, with tree roots growing through the wings and what remained of its mottled original paint. You could have taken my money if you had bet me that one day I would see it again like this!

▶

Classic Fighter. Is there a more purposeful looking fighting aircraft than the Bf109? Square corners and a blunt nose topped off with machine guns, this ruthless little aircraft arguably 'edged it' as the ultimate fighter in the battles of 1940 due to the fact that it could sling so much more lead at its opponents in the same amount of time. John Romain flies the stunning and original Battle of Britain yellow-nosed E-model in both these shots, whilst Alan Walker pilots the predatory Hurricane off his wing with a glistening coast below.

◀

The shape that may have just saved the World. R.J. Mitchell's design genius is never more evident than when viewed as the Spitfire's planform.

▶

Frasca's Flying Tiger. I first met Rudy Frasca back in 1991 when I photographed his Spitfire Mk XVIII in the UK. He invited me to his Museum in Champaign Illinois where we flew together again with his P-40 Kittyhawk. Rudy was a steady and smooth pilot of many years experience. He could calmly place that aeroplane to the inch, which was encouraging as the shark's mouth artwork looked threatening enough as it was!

▲

Spitfire Mk Ia, AR213, once the mount of legendary Battle of Britain ace Ginger Lacey, peels away to reveal the planform that will bring a tear to the eye of any lion-hearted Englishman.

▶

The Master. I often heard World War 2 veterans say that Ray Hanna was the master Spitfire pilot and hopefully this shot may go some way to illustrate their point. I've heard comments that this shot was faked. I hate to disappoint anybody, but I was there and I can tell you it's real. With impeccable timing, Ray 'drove' that aircraft into the tiniest 'window' of sky to get the perfect position for my viewpoint. What a pilot.

◀

National Icons. Before Paul Allen, the microsoft co-founder, shipped his beautiful Spitfire Mk V restoration back to the US, I was asked to shoot the aircraft over the UK. For some reason we were drawn to the White Cliffs! The symbolic power of this national landmark is palpable today, what it must have meant back in 1939-45 one can only wonder.

◀

It takes just one look at a B-17 and I can hear the opening line from William Wyler's classic 1943 movie 'Memphis Belle': 'This is a battlefield' says the narrator, as masses of Flying Fortresses run up and hedgerows swirl in prop wash in rural picturesque England. For many people worldwide, the US 8th Air Force operations from East Anglia define the American air war effort during the conflict. I have flown many photo sorties from former World War 2 airfields: Duxford, North Weald, Fowlmere, Biggin Hill, as well as Deenethorpe, a former B-17 base. Luckily not only do a few of these airfields still exist, but so do the aircraft. The B-17 is rarer than you might think, however there is no finer sight than a Fortress aloft and here 'Yankee Lady' is captured where she was always meant to be, set high in a skyscape loaded with clouds.

▶

There are moments in life that jar your perspective. When planning a shoot to pair these two iconic aircraft, I inadvertently created such a moment. The intention was to provide a direct comparison of the airframes, but I also thought I might document the tail chases that prove so popular at air shows. Looking out on a 109 chasing a P-51 (and vice versa), I became witness to a chilling 'window through time': No longer was this Mark Hanna chasing Brian Smith in two air show machines, but a disconcerting view on the experiences of those young pilots who flew, fought and died 60 years before.

◀ British Bulldog. Bud Granley is the pilot sliding the Flying Heritage Hurricane into our six o'clock. The bulldog artwork looks just about ready to bop me on the nose, such is the clarity of the Canon lenses.

▲ A Corsair's unique bent wing can make you look twice. Hopefully one upside down will make you look three times. I guess this is the true definition of an inverted gull-wing!

▲

'Angels Playmate' — what a great name for a Mustang. Lee Lauderback does the honours in a late Floridian afternoon.

◄

Stephen Grey, the leading light of The Fighter Collection, takes their recently restored (at the time) rare C model Mustang into the vertical. Norman Lees was the camera-ship pilot. Norman was unfortunately to lose his life in a Spitfire training accident in 2000. Norman was very much a guiding light in the early days and was hugely influential in helping me understand the challenges of warbird photography. More Morecombe and Wise than Butch and Sundance, we were firm friends. The world shines slightly less bright without Norman in it.

►

Aces and Legends. I always endeavour to tie my photographs to stories that tell the experiences of those who flew the machines in combat. This image will always stand out for me in the fact that it not only shows two P-51s in tight dramatic formation, but remarkably the two pilots are aces Gen Chuck Yeager and Col Bud Anderson, flying the mounts that represented their aircraft from World War 2! At the time, both pilots were in their eighties, but for them close formation flying was as natural as ever. What supreme airmanship from two legends.

Pete Kynsey nestled atop the mighty Jug. This shot looks quite 'summery', but it was taken very late in the year and on a cold, cold day. The camera-ship was a Beech Baron. I took the luggage door off as the aircraft was having an interior refit. I knew the angle I was after but once airborne couldn't quite see it. So I told the two pilots up front that I was taking off my headset and going 'outside'. I very carefully put one arm out, then my head and then the other arm with the camera tied to it. I was out to my ribcage. What's that like? Loud, tremendously loud is the first shock. If Spinal Tap's amp went to 11, the outside of a Baron at 180 knots is a 12. I had split plate goggles on but even with those the tears were being sucked off my eyes! I could just see watery images of a black and white checkerboard, quite close. I pulled myself together and focussed both mind and camera and got the shot. Now to get back in. Easier said than done. Both elbows were outside and so I had no leverage to get back through the tiny doorway. Also no headset to plead for assistance. The guys up front, with the heater on, told me after that they thought I must be getting great stuff as 'he's been out there for ages'. I tapped SOS with my feet to try to get assistance to be pulled back in. No luck. I was getting tired too. It was searingly cold besides the battering and noise. One last big effort. I am not sure how but it worked and I retracted back into the fuselage. The two pilots sensed the lack of drag that I had been causing and looked back. I gave a slightly frost-bitten thumbs up.

All the shots I take are real and have not been created in Photoshop. Sometimes, though, elements come together that make others question the image's validity. This was one such shot. It shows Pete Kynsey in The Fighter Collection's P-47G Thunderbolt. As we 'weedled' through ever massing clouds, this image presented itself. Click. The frame before and the frame after just don't have the power that the centred thunderhead cloud brings to this image. Later, a pilot friend of mine commented that he really liked the picture, but 'it's a shame that it was faked'! He thought the aircraft was over Duxford but that the clouds were from somewhere over the Pacific!

▲ Classic Foes. There is a power to imagery combining former enemies. Whilst I don't want to make light and 're-enact' war, sometimes the most compelling way to make a point is to do just that. Here Planes of Fame's genuine A6M Zero shares the skies with a P-40 Warhawk.

▲ Catwalks and Runways. This is as close as it must get for an aviation photographer to work with supermodels. Not that the pilots John Romain and Lee Proudfoot aren't fine specimens of our species, but I am of course referring to the pure beauty of the two Spitfire Mk Is. Words cannot describe the sight of these machines flying together up close and personal. You can almost hear Churchill's words on the note of the Merlins.

◀

'B' is for Blenheim and Beautiful. One of the true standout restorations of the warbird World has been the three incarnations of The Aircraft Restoration Company's Bristol Blenheim. Recently returned to the skies as a Mk I, this aircraft is simply regal, an art deco masterpiece in metal and rivets. Every time you see this aircraft I implore you to take a moment to think of the brave crews that held the line in 1939/40.

▶

Flying Heritage Collection's IL-2 Sturmovik is something else to behold. Former Snowbird pilot Ross Granley was behind the complicated and heavy stick for the photo-sortie. He flew this legendary tank buster impeccably. Amazingly you can still see bullet holes in the lower cowls and during the shoot I noticed zigzags of ricocheted ground fire cut into the top cowling. This aircraft was there for sure, fighting for Mother Russia.

▶ Grumman 'Cats' are rare beasts from World War 2, and 'beast' is the best word for this machine. Strong, tough and outhouse-like, the Hellcat was the right machine to fight it out in the arduous Pacific campaign. With a 19:1 kill ratio, this aircraft was the one you wanted on your side. Such is the originality of Paul Allen's FHC F6F-5, that the propeller blades actually have consecutive serial numbers. It is 'all-motor' and that is what I was striving to capture here.

▲ Break Break Go! Tom Blair an American collector has a penchant for Spitfires. These are two of the three he had at the time. Cliff Spink and Dave Ratcliffe go their separate ways in picture perfect fashion.

ADRENALINE JUNKIES

THE COLOUR OF FLIGHT

Flight to make the heart beat faster. Filling the skies with skill, colour, noise and smoke is what these pilots live for. Brightening the summer skies for every aviation enthusiast and flying close to the edge gives everyone a rush.

◀◀ *Previous Page*

The Matadors were a Red Bull-sponsored team of Xtremeair XA41s flown by Paul Bonhomme and Steve Jones. Aerobatic aircraft break the rules of 'conventional' flight and with two uber-talented pilots behind the stick, then creating imagery to showcase that becomes a challenge in itself, despite the skills of those involved. Interestingly I found I was trying to rebalance myself in the camera-ship, as the differing angles of the subject to the airflow made you feel you must be going in another direction!

This photo just says 'Yippeee!' to me whenever I see it. If you ever want to understand what flying can mean to a person or the excellence involved, then just look at this image. It's all fun, but all business. Precision flying and the spirit of Andreya Wharry, the wing walker, just jumps through the lens.

David Gilmour of Pink Floyd fame had a collection of aircraft based at North Weald in the 1990s. Amongst his aircraft was the Folland Gnat in pre-Red Arrows colours, a bright colourful scheme of the CFS 'Yellowjacks'. Inspired by Arthur Gibson's Red Arrows shots from the 1960-80s, I like to see this as an homage to the master of Gnat photography. An iconic jet whisking off into the blue on a comet tail of jet thrust.

⏪ *Previous Spread*

Up Close. Flying with the Red Arrows is something that cannot be described in words alone. You need lots of handwaving and to drink decaff so you might actually speak at a rate that others might understand. Whilst the most recognisable image is the nine jets stuck on a sheet of glass rolling in the blue, it is the 'pilot's eye' view that truly reveals the ultimate professionalism of these elite flyers. So close you could almost touch, but hopefully not.

Extreme Machine. Blackie 'Schwarz' is chief rotary pilot for the Flying Bulls and flies the Bolkow 105 in a full aerobatic regime. Here he is seen doing something you wouldn't expect high in the Austrian Alps. I was perched out the side of a Bell 47 on a gin clear morning to shoot the Bo105 atop a ridgeline, but as I am scared of heights my heart was in my mouth and all I wanted to do was crawl into the back of the bubble. However, when I saw Blackie doing this outside the door I thought that it might be time to 'man up' and get the shot. I did a bit of a Pope John Paul when we landed, but get extra satisfaction from these images knowing that I overcame a truly gripping fear to get them.

The Sea Vixen is such a fabulous looking machine. Respelendent in the red and yellow colours of its final service days at RAF Llanbedr and piloted by Dan Griffith, the aircraft looks half aircraft, half spaceship.

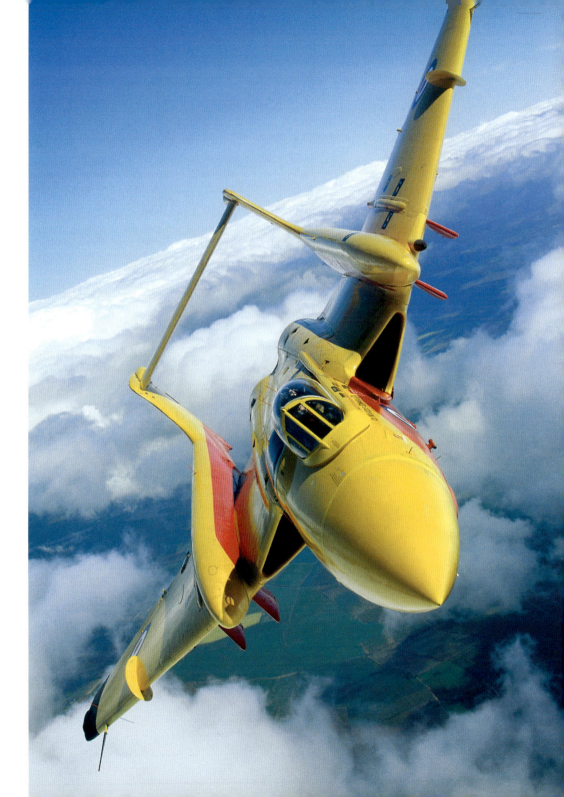

INTO THE BLUE

CIVIL AND COMMERCIAL

As the turbine powerhouse behind global economics, or just the essential style statement for the rich and famous, the fabulously-engineered machines of the civil aircraft world have changed all of our lives.

◀◀ *Previous Page*

The Rocket. On the day the new British Airways scheme was unveiled, Concorde was launched from Heathrow to show the World's press the new colours. As part of the marketing plan I was sat in a Learjet over Wiltshire to get film and stills of the aircraft in its bright new livery. Unfortunately on the day of the launch the weather was bad and the ceiling was about 32,000ft. We couldn't film looking down as all you could see was the windscreen of the SST against a flat white cloud layer. Capt Mike Bannister suggested we film the aircraft climbing up and away but the Lear was pretty near its camera-system limit, with its potential to literally freeze up at that height. So we sat at our altitude behind Concorde and Capt Bannister 'buried his foot in the Axminster', to borrow a motoring phrase. The Lear shook as if it was coming apart (it actually might have been) and we could hear the four Olympus engines torturing the thin air by cooking it and chucking it out the back. Just as if Jean Luc-Picard had said 'Make it so', the World's most beautiful aircraft zipped off into the upper reaches of the atmosphere, leaving that normal little sportscar of a jet, the Lear, feeling somewhat pedestrian.

These two photos get a lot of 'How did you shoot that, are they real?' comments. As to how the image was shot, I could tell you, but then I would have to kill you. Suffice to say that Concorde pilot Jock Lowe was there, I was there and so was my trusty Canon, so it's real for sure. I feel very privileged to have shot air-to-air with Concorde for British Airways on behalf of the then marketing manager Andy Patsalides. He was the perfect client and let experience take the lead where it needed, to help him create a wide portfolio of images.

▲ Gulfstream offers a range of jets just in case you need one... or two! There is an elegant stark beauty to biz-jets. Every line is both efficient and stylish. Framed against the lush Oregon coast, two of these high roller's favourites move through the air with sleek grace.

◄ I used to watch the RAF Dominies fly into Northolt when I was a child, so getting to shoot the type in its latest reincarnation for Hawker Beechcraft was a real treat. The sun wrapped its dying rays around the aircraft on what was close to a perfect shoot.

◀

Pictured over Lake Powell in Nevada, the breathtaking desert and water location provided a perfect foil for the neat lines of the Gulfstream.

▶

Shooting for TAG Aviation out of Geneva was a real highlight for me, simply because the backgrounds were astounding wherever you looked. This Lear 35 set amid the Alps is one of my favourite photos, the smooth man-crafted curves of the aircraft looking vulnerable among the immense grandeur of nature.

▶

Sleek Sunset. A flight in a Gulfstream G550 seems like a perfect way to end the day.

▲ Ironically, I first flew on a Boeing 747 going to a meeting to talk about photographing one. However, the 'gentle giant' had captured my imagination throughout my childhood. After all, the Jumbo is only one of a few airliners that the general public can pick out of a line up, so naturally it must be a classic. The -400 version has an elegance over the -100/200, with the winglets and longer bump. I requested a formation pilot from the British Airways 747 fleet and with his Harrier background he seemingly forgot he had 200ft of aircraft behind him rather than the usual 35ft of the Harrier. His skill in positioning this mighty aircraft was a testament to both the RAF's and BA's training as well as the skill of the Boeing engineers.

◀ When British Airways bought the B777, they took delivery of the GE90-powered prototype. Due to requirements to use the images big, we had to shoot through clear air and not through a periscope system such as a Learjet. So I found myself drowning in the sound that is B-25 flying. This example had a big old tail port and the former US Marine pilot flying the 777 knew how to tuck in. Later, the B-25 pilot said he could feel the 'bow-wave' of the airliner pushing us forward! Looking like a killer whale due to the old BA paint scheme, this shot proved satisfying as it so emphasised the massive new generation engines that would define ETOPS.

▲ When Virgin Atlantic repainted its A330 fleet in a slick new scheme, I was asked to film motion pictures and stills for the marketing campaign. Now, the A330 is not just long, it is very long, so it is quite challenging to shoot, but caught at the correct angle it has the lines of a powerful classic.

▶ Rather bizarrely, but more typical than you might think of people that fly, I am scared of heights. Also I used to be terribly scared of flying, especially on airliners. No view forward, no ejector seat, no parachute… you get the drift. Anyhow, it was once I started to photograph airliners that I realised what immense engineering achievements they are. Reliable, powerful and so strong. Take this photo of the stunningly-painted Virgin 747-400 with its nose pointed to the heavens. It easily out-climbed the jet we were in. Now, relax, sit back and enjoy the flight…

▲ When settling down for the in-flight entertainment in an airliner, it is so difficult to imagine that you are sitting in a tin-tube miles above the Earth. I like to think that this angle gives an appreciation of the reality of what we all take for granted and that the BA 757 is in full ownership of the painter's pallet that we call the sky.

◀ DAS Air Cargo commissioned me to shoot their freight operation that utilised the DC-10 airframe. There are not a lot of pilots who have experience in close formation flying in a large airliner, so CAA training captain Dan Griffith was sanctioned to pilot the big tri-jet for the shoot. Dan is a truly gifted test pilot with over 200 types in his logbook, including warbirds and fast jets. His formation flying is text book, which he may well have written.

▲ Austrian Airlines is another Boeing customer that bought the mighty 777. Capturing an aircraft during its delivery flight is always a challenge, but it is the only time when it will have no passengers on-board, which allows me to get close. The low winter sun sends shards of pine forest shadows across the landscape, which lends speed to the image.

▶ In the heyday of Duxford being the mainstay of the British warbird industry, I met many interesting and amazing pilots who flew displays in World War 2 aircraft at the weekend and then put a tie on and flew an airliner the following day. Putting a tie on seems to stop you wanting to barrel roll or loop the aircraft you are in. A few pilots championed my cause to get their airlines some of the same type of imagery that we were getting with warbirds. Alan Walker and Paul Chaplin both flew for the Old Flying Machine Company, but wore an Air 2000 tie for real jobs. Naturally we found ourselves creating some innovative ideas and this is one of my favourites. Paul is the man behind the yoke and I love the nonchalance of the co-pilot looking out — he's actually keeping a beady eye on potential traffic, but that doesn't come across in this. So next time you are eating a chicken dinner out of a foil dish on the way to Malaga, just remember that the pilots up front may have flown a Spitfire at the weekend.

WIND IN THE WIRES

CLASSIC BRITISH BIPLANES

Huge wooden propellers swinging at the cool blue air and shuddering fabric stretched over wood, created flight as harmonized as the wind whistling through bracing wires. Biplane technology, or more accurately the lack of it, has a timeless appeal and the British were rather good at it, so therefore celebrated with a boldness of colour set on silver doped linen in a way that lightens the heart.

◀◀ *Previous Page*

I once quipped that the Swordfish only needed one wing, the other was to lift the spirits of the crews that flew these obsolete machines into the fury of Axis naval gunfire. Piled atop the Royal Navy Historic Flight's Swordfish, this crew thankfully only have to deliver this Tinfish to an adoring air show crowd.

▲ Scourge of the Jasta. The SE5a in many ways broke the mould of early World War 1 fighters in that it actually looked like it meant business. The thin square set wings and the blunt nose carry a solidity that hint at its purposeful performance.

◀ With a Rothschild mansion below nestling in the trees gently brushed with an evening light, this Sopwith 1 1/2 Strutter setting perfectly evokes feelings that were directly in contrast to the horror of the trenches it might have patrolled during The Great War.

The devil is in the detail. **Howell Davies'** Hawker Demon is a meticulous and glorious restoration of a very rare bird. Stu Goldspink is one of the UK's most experienced early aircraft specialists. We have worked together many times and he holds a torch for close formation flying in aircraft with 'interesting' handling. The huge wooden propeller chopping at the air does grab your attention, but you couldn't ask for a finer wingman. Just look at this machine it's fabulous.

My father's favourite aircraft was the Gloster Gladiator. He watched them perform at Empire Air Days at Northolt and Hendon, three tied together with ribbon, looping. I was agog as a child at his descriptions of the derring-do of air show pilots. His love was passed on to me and luckily, Stephen Grey had not only the love of the type but the passion to put one back in the skies. Now where is my box of ribbons?

▲ If the engineering issue of trying to slide an airframe through the air unnoticed whilst having to deal with lots of problems, like multiple wings and the drag from wires being pulled by a less powerful engine, helped create the beautiful lines of the inter-war fighters, then it might almost be worth it! The Fighter Collection's Hawker Nimrod carries aloft another version of the audacious colour schemes worn by 1930s RAF squadrons.

◄ Perfect evening for a spot of flying you might say. John Romain is seen here puttering above the English countryside in an Avro 504K. An interwar trainer, this machine was the first mount of many future aces and heroes of World War 2.

GODS OF THUNDER

MODERN MILITARY AIR POWER

Nothing says the projection of global air power more than a modern military jet, whether that is a transport aircraft heaving supplies or fighter jets skimming the stratosphere at the speed of cool. Either way, fight's on!

◀◀ *Previous Page*

Formation breaks look great with fighter jets as all the angles of airframe and flightpaths generate a moment that can't really be matched in other arenas of aviation photography. Getting a good break is hard, but the perfect break is, well harder. This gets pretty close, with Wg Cdr Toby Craig, Boss of that most historic of RAF fighter Squadrons, No 17, calling the shots to get the image. Prior to the sortie, I walked the squadron's halls and offices which are bedecked with bits of Luftwaffe aircraft brought down by '17' during the Battle of Britain. It helps get your game face on. How ironic that just a few decades and a few hundred miles away, the victims of such trophy gathering are now flying the same aircraft as '17' and as friends not enemies in the modern day Luftwaffe.

The Man in the Bubble. As the pilot is generally busy actually doing something useful during take off, this is the one time I point the camera inwards to take 'pilot' photos. I guess this is the ultimate selfie, but it does put the human element amongst all the high-tech wizardry. This shot was taken as an F-16D made a particularly impressive climb-out from Graf Ignatievo, Bulgaria. All of a sudden the camera weighed three times heavier than usual, but thankfully you can't see my gritted teeth behind the oxygen mask.

Don't Mess with Texas or 'Mongo', who was flying this F-16C of the Ellington Field based Houston ANG. 'Mongo like G!', in deference to the 'Blazing Saddles' character was the order of the day. Not only am I fascinated by the twirling 'fluff' atop the wings, but the vapour spirals off the AMRAAM and the twist of the missile as the G-Force loads up. 'Dibbsy' and 'Mongo' both like G!

F-16C Viper, 308th FS

F-16C Viper, 308th FS

F-16C Viper pair, 62nd FS

F-15A Eagle, 199th FS

▲ Sir Isaac Newton meets the F-16. Sometimes it just looks like fun — and for me this captures the delight of flying. Powering through towering cumulus on a steamy afternoon above Bulgaria, this F-16CJ pilot doesn't seem to care much for apples or which way they fall .

▶ Panther Pounce. Lt Col 'Opie' Stewart flew many of the photo-sorties for my Viper Force book at Luke AFB. When the 63rd FS Panthers were being retired, he finally managed to switch from being behind the lens to in front of it, as he was on the 63rd for one of its final photo-calls over the breathtaking Arizona landscape. 'Opie' was (and still is) a very cool customer. I learned a lot about global SA (situational awareness) from this man when he was wrangling the various assets during shoots we undertook. Whether low over the range or operating in the extremely high areas where the blue sky starts to turn a bit more black, he was always in control. I recall one moment at the top of a very high lofting manoeuvre where weather had taken us forever higher. The jet went very 'light' at the top of the arc, and my camera, arms and legs went a bit floaty. Time to be concerned about being ballistic? Apparently not as the cry 'Pigs in Spaaaace!' came from the front of the bubble. Giggling in zero G is actually fun. No Muppets when 'Opie' was honcho though.

▲ Above the Rest. The F-22 Raptor sparks many a debate, on cost and relevance, but talking with the pilots and seeing the viewable data on its performance, you cannot argue that it is one hell of an aircraft. One pilot put it to me succinctly: 'If it comes down to it and we go to the fight, then people will only realise what we have when every F-22 guy comes back an ace from that first mission.' 'Lite' Gray in a 95th FS Tyndall AFB F-22 makes his own weather.

▶ Star-spangled Raptor! Air dominance Raptor-style. 'Stiffler' Gration pilots his Elmendorf-based 302nd FS F-22 through a freezing Alaskan sky, pistols drawn looking for 'trade'.

▲ The Dragon. Trials out of Holloman AFB with a light grey daylight scheme for the F-117 resulted in a name change as Nighthawk was not really appropriate. So the project was called Dragon. I personally loved this scheme and it was a lot easier to photograph than an all black jet!

Looking like an alien craft over Mars, this 9th FS F-117A Nighthawk looks every bit as menacing as it should near its home base at Holloman AFB. The aircraft's stealth properties needed particular and regular maintenance by the Materials Application Repair Section (M.A.R.S.), appropriately referred to as Martians. British exchange pilot Flt Lt Richie Matthews was the pilot, himself a former Red (Arrow), so this whole Mars-themed caption is working out.

Air dominance Raptor-style. A Tyndal-based 95th FS F-22 wheels through the skies over a shadow-spattered Gulf of Mexico.

▲

The Eagle was designed in the early 1970s and coupled the idea that to make a good fighter all you needed was a bucket load of thrust, a huge radar and an airframe that was large enough to carry the fuel and missiles necessary to the enemy. They were right. Throwing in the fact that it was highly manoeuvrable just enabled them to put a capital G in it's nickname 'WGASF' — Worlds Greatest Air Superiority Fighter. You can smell the testosterone and feel the heat. The Brits have a great way of understating things and whilst our American cousins prefer the more manly term 'reheat' or 'Blower' for afterburner thrust, I like our term — 'Carrot Power'! So behold two Hawaiian F-15As in full carrot power set against a beautiful pacific evening sky.

▲

Dangling upside down over the Gulf of Mexico is fun, even more fun when a Raptor is revealing all those complex airframe shapes below you. The skill in the positioning was down to 'Roman', my Eagle camera-ship pilot. Why 'Roman'? He didn't look Mediterranean. The call-sign 'Roman' was bestowed upon him for life after a display of missile firing where he unleashed so much firepower that he resembled a one-man fireworks display, Roman Candle. It stuck. Great guy, great flying.

▶

If you had to ask me to choose one favourite photo… well I couldn't answer that. However this is pretty much up there. It was an idea that my F-15 pilot friend and later to be co-author, 'Cricket' Renner had. He spent his Eagle days training to be the best and this often would include BFM, or basic fighter manoeuvres. Another slightly tongue in cheek term for this art form is Big Flipping Mystery! Anyhow BFM starts with the 'Merge'. The two combatants fly at each other head on, and as soon as they pass 'Fights On!' Cricket suggested we try to capture this. The things I love about this image are, firstly, there is a lot going on — flares popping, the jet is in afterburner, the second combatant is pulling hard to get an advantage and thankfully his flares spread perfectly around the tank of the foreground subject whilst twirling to show how hard he is pulling. Secondly, this image is not taken on a zoom lens or with motor drive. Its shot on a 24-70mm set at about 1-to-1 with your eye. Yes, that close. No Photoshop, no zoom, just a split second of being able to witness the fighter pilot doing what they do. Canon autofocus man, I owe you a beer. EOS autofocus is faster than an Eagle can blink.

F-22 Raptor, 302nd FS/90th FS

F-16C Viper, 147th FW

F-18C Hornet, VFA-125

F-15C Eagle, 19th FS

▲ This was a 'new' idea for a break, something I scribbled on the back of a napkin on the flight to Texas. I was desperately wanting to create a new style of break other than the 'one goes one way, ones goes the other'. I considered that this new manoeuvre could be achieved safely and with the crews signing off on it, we flew the profile. I was (still am) chuffed with the result.

▶ Two F-18E Super Hornets from the VFA-147 Argonauts cover the skies above the Sierra Nevadas out of Lemoore NAS. With the sun setting I thought it couldn't get any more perfect until I noticed the fog rolling through the gaps in the mountain crests. Epic.

▲ The Mirror Breaks. I had an idea for a shot to create a dynamic split but with a difference. It took a long time to work out how to achieve this and the pilots, 'Otto' and 'Burn', worked diligently with me to fly the profile. Time at the briefing table is well spent. We attempted it once and thanks to digital I knew we got it first time. I don't think I would have survived trying this with Kodachrome and then having to wait 10 days to see if it was in the can!

▲ 'Doc' Ellis CO of the Emerald Knights in full A/B, loosing off a 2,000lb-er over the range. Another day in the office for a member of the Viper set.

▶ Crew of Two. Seymour Johnson-based F-15E Strike Eagle, pilot and WSO evident in this close plan view.

▲ This image is one of my personal favourites. The C-17 is an incredible aircraft, I love working with them and the crews that operate them. Their work is not always glamorous but it's vital and the machine is a wonder. It's a very dynamic machine and I was pleased to capture one over Alaska with low pressure fluff signifying the lift of the wing working as the big machine sweeps down a glacial valley. This is very much business as usual for the Globemaster fleet.

◀ The Hawaiian Air National Guard operates many types from the place that man must have had trouble describing before coming up with the word 'paradise'. The in-house heavy lift component of supplying the United States military assets through the Pacific corridor falls to the 154th Wing's C-17s. Shot at sunset over the West coast of Kauai, I remember being all discombobulated by the fact we were above cloud (typically high in the tropics), but still level with the cliffs. The Loadmaster shouted in my ear that the cliffs were over 2,000ft high. The winds were strong and I noticed that the subject's engine pods were swinging independently and the wing flexing to ride the bumps. I commented on this to the pilot after landing, stating that the Loadie and I were glad we weren't on their jet. He said they were looking at us watching out tail thrash from side to side and saying the same. No wonder I was doing a Hula on the ramp whilst shooting.

◀ ▲ The Phantom could never be accused of being shy, but it is retiring. After decades of eminent service, the USAF is finally bring to an end the F-4's career. This version, the QF-4, is part of the 53rd WEG at Tyndall, known as the 'Rhino' by some. This aircraft is also being flown by the unit's CO, who rather conveniently has the call sign 'Rhino', so that makes for an easy caption. Set at altitude amid an early morning sky brimming with cumulus, this SE Asia Heritage-marked Phantom was a career high to shoot.

◀ ▲ The 160th Special Operations Aviation Regiment is the US military's way of getting things done quietly and efficiently. Working with the Special Forces of many nations, the 'Nightstalkers Don't Quit', as per their motto. Operating many modified helicopters in the most challenging of conditions is a given for the pilots and crews of the 160th. Sinister is not the word for the mighty MH-47s and MH-60s they operate. These machines look like they could kick-in the Terminator's door and make it see reason. The brutish proportions of these 'helos' are only matched by the tenacity and bravery of the crews.

▲ I always thought that the T-38 looked slinky enough that you should try and buy it a drink! These gloss black Aggressors of the 2nd FS definitely look like a 1950's movie star with their corseted area-ruled waistlines. Col 'Bud' Wyler and his roster of highly-experienced fighter pilots are set up on a daily basis to challenge the Tyndall Raptors .

▶ The lead pilot of the Viggen formation asked me if I was British. After I replied in the affirmative, he tapped the screen when we were reviewing the images just shot on a cold and clear Östersund morning and said with a wry smile, 'OK, then say we were Harrier hunting'.

◀ ▲ I love art, and aviation art. I did try my hand at painting once, but it took a terribly long time. I was shocked. So when someone stuck a camera in my hand I realised that I could create an image that while it might not be 'art-art' only took me 1/250th sec to generate. Occasionally I look at an aviation painting and wince at how good it is. Should I have considered my decision more? Then over Bulgaria you are sitting next to a MiG-29, that beautiful blue grey shark of the skies, and this happens. Greens and blues by nature, offset with silver shimmers on water. Then mix-in a MiG 21 (above right) inked out against a swirl of sunset tones. Luckily I had a helmet on or I would have cut off my ear.

GODS OF THUNDER | 103

RAF Harrier T10 backseat
RAF Jaguar GR1 over the Orkneys
RAF Harrier GR7 SNEB launching

RAF Tornado F3s

Maritime Strike. Packing two Sea Eagle anti-shipping missiles and Hindenburg drop tanks, this No 12 Squadron Tornado GR1B RAF looks just as menacing as it actually is. With its two RB199 turbofans force-feeding the heavens into a rarefied-air mix of blue and purple afterburning, this 'GR1B' with it's wings slewed back heads out to patrol the shores of Scotland.

The Mighty Hunter. The Nimrod R1 was a highly classified aircraft used by the RAF up until 2011. Wg Cdr Richie Matthews, a former Red Arrows and Jaguar pilot, was the unit's Boss in its last couple of years. Therefore, when permission was granted to shoot the aircraft, I knew we would get some good results. The Nimrod airframe has a sci-fi look to it. It is retro and yet brand new all at once. The underbelly prickles with electronic gizmos trained on all sorts of signals and beeps that might give away untoward thoughts of potential enemies.

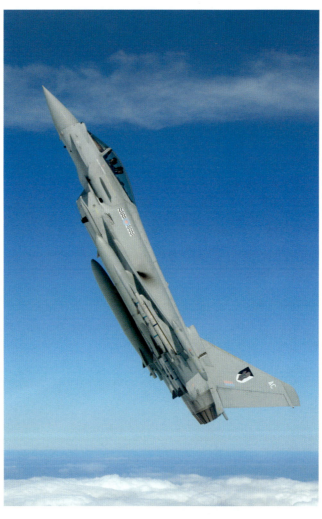

▲ Just Aggressive, No Passive. The Eurofighter Typhoon has taken the RAF's capability to another level and with lots of thrust a big wing and a highly sophisticated flight control system, the earth can so easily be put where you want it to be.

▶ Flt Lt Stefan Wurwal of No1 Squadron whips this Typhoon GR4 on its back with a full load of air-to-air mischief.

With over 1,100 sorties flown I can honestly still say I never take anything for granted and am eternally grateful to those who make all this possible. Here are three 'proud to be British' stand out moments. The Vulcan to the Skies Trust Vulcan being flown by 'Mr Black Buck' mission himself, Martin Withers. A stormy winter sea pounding the Orkneys' coastline, whilst a Jaguar GR1 of No XVI Squadron RAF rolls in, carrying a 1,000lb Paveway on the centreline, burners aglow and the wing tips tearing at the air. Dave Southwood sitting on a column of R-R Avon thrust high over Boscombe Down in the prettiest Hunter I ever saw.

Star Wars Canyon. Flt Lt 'Tess' Tickle takes us skywalking in a No 16 Squadron Sepecat Jaguar GR1 through Glen Tilt valley in Scotland.

SUBSCRIBE & SAVE
TO YOUR FAVOURITE AVIATION MAGAZINE

Britain's Top Selling Aviation Monthly

FLYPAST is internationally regarded as the magazine for aviation history and heritage. Having pioneered coverage of this fascinating world of 'living history' since 1980, FlyPast still leads the field today. Each issue is packed with news and features on warbird preservation and restoration, museums, and the airshow scene. Subjects regularly profiled include British and American aircraft type histories, as well as those of squadrons and units from World War One to the Cold War.

The World's Number One Military Aviation Magazine

Published monthly, **AIRFORCES MONTHLY** is devoted entirely to modern military aircraft and their air arms. It has built up a formidable reputation worldwide by reporting from places not generally covered by other military magazines. Its world news is the best around, covering all aspects of military aviation, region by region; offering features on the strengths of the world's air forces, their conflicts, weaponry and exercises.

Requirements for app: registered iTunes account on Apple iPhone 3G, 3GS, 4S, 5, iPod Touch or iPad 1, 2 or 3. Internet connection required for initial download. Published by Key Publishing Ltd. The entire contents of these titles are © copyright 2015. All rights reserved. App prices subject to change.